Green STEAM

EARTH-FRIENDLY
SCIENCE
CRAFTS

Veronica Thompson

Lerner Publications ◆ Minneapolis

Lerner Publications Company
A division of Lerner Publishing Group, Inc.
241 First Avenue North
Minneapolis, MN 55401 USA

For reading levels and more information, look up this title at www.lernerbooks.com.

Main body text set in Avenir LT Pro 12/16.
Typeface provided by Linotype AG.

Photo Acknowledgments
The images in this book are used with the permission of: © cosmaa/Shutterstock Images, p. 1 (Earth icon); © Stilesta/Shutterstock Images, pp. 1, 3, 9, 11, 13, 15, 17, 19, 21, 23, 25, 27, 28 (border design element); © Dragon Images/Shutterstock Images, p. 4 (kids); © Leigh Prather/Shutterstock Images, p. 4 (test tubes); © Mama Belle Love kids/Shutterstock Images, p. 5; © Elena Elisseeva/Shutterstock Images, p. 6 (top); © Bunwit Unseree/Shutterstock Images, p. 6 (bag); © TayaCho/iStockphoto, p. 6 (jar); © Aphisit Ragput/Shutterstock Images, p. 7 (jar); © Sylvie Bouchard/Shutterstock Images, p. 7 (background); Veronica Thompson, pp. 8, 9 (top), 9 (center), 9 (bottom), 10, 11 (top), 11 (center), 11 (bottom), 12, 13 (top), 13 (center), 13 (bottom), 14, 15 (top), 15 (center), 15 (bottom), 16, 17 (top), 17 (center), 17 (bottom), 18, 19 (top), 19 (center), 19 (bottom), 20, 21 (top), 21 (center), 21 (bottom), 22, 23 (top), 23 (center), 23 (bottom), 24, 25 (top), 25 (center), 25 (bottom), 26, 27 (top), 27 (center), 27 (bottom), 28 (top), 28 (center), 28 (bottom); © Curly Pat/Shutterstock Images, pp. 9, 11, 13, 15, 17, 19, 21, 23, 25, 27, 28 (design element); © Chones/Shutterstock Images, p. 29 (top); © monticello/Shutterstock Images, p. 29 (bottom); © mikeledray/Shutterstock Images, p. 30; © Castleski/Shutterstock Images, p. 31; © NASA/JPL/University of Arizona, p. 32 (top); Courtesy Veronica Thompson, p. 32 (bottom)

Front cover: Veronica Thompson (main); © cosmaa/Shutterstock Images (Earth icon)
Back cover: © Curly Pat/Shutterstock Images (background design element); © Stilesta/Shutterstock Images (border design element)

Library of Congress Cataloging-in-Publication Data

Names: Thompson, Veronica, 1989– author.
Title: Earth-friendly science crafts / by Veronica Thompson.
Description: Minneapolis, MN : Lerner Publications, [2019] | Series: Green STEAM | Includes bibliographical references and index. | Audience: Ages 8-11. | Audience: Grade 4 to 6.
Identifiers: LCCN 2017059751 (print) | LCCN 2017057040 (ebook) | ISBN 9781541524231 (eb pdf) | ISBN 9781541524163 (lb : alk. paper) | ISBN 9781541527829 (pb : alk. paper)
Subjects: LCSH: Handicraft—Juvenile literature. | Science—Experiments—Juvenile literature.
Classification: LCC TT160 (print) | LCC TT160 .T36728 2019 (ebook) | DDC 745.5—dc23

LC record available at https://lccn.loc.gov/2017059751

Manufactured in the United States of America
1-44504-34760-4/24/2018

CONTENTS

Scan QR codes throughout for step-by-step pictures of each craft.

CRAFT WITH SCIENCE!

Crafting gets more exciting with science! Use science concepts to make crafts that fizz, change states of matter, and more. You don't need lab equipment to make these cool creations. Repurposed and recycled items are perfect for science crafts, and they're good for the earth too.

Get ready to create your own Earth-friendly crafts with science!

CHOOSING MATERIALS

When you're gathering things to repurpose, it's okay to be picky. For example, avoid bent bottle caps or crushed plastic bottles. And ask an adult for permission before dyeing clothing.

CLEAN MACHINE

Recycled or reused materials may be dirty or carry leftover food. Give these materials a good scrub before you craft with them! Rinse out glass jars and plastic bottles, and wash and dry fabric items.

STAY SAFE!

Some crafts in this book require sharp tools or powerful dyes and liquids. Ask for an adult's help when using these items:

- craft knife
- hot glue gun
- nail polish
- powder fabric dye

SOLAR SYSTEM PINS

Repurpose bottle caps into pins of planets, moons, and more!

MATERIALS
~ recycled bottle caps
~ paint in different colors
~ paintbrushes
~ clear nail polish
~ hot glue gun & glue sticks
~ pin backs

Scan the QR code for more photos.

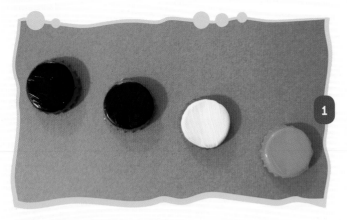

1 Paint two bottle caps blue, one white, and one orange.

EARTH

2 Paint green shapes on a blue cap as Earth's continents.

CRESCENT MOON

3 Paint a white arc on one third of the second blue cap. Paint small gray circles on the white arc as craters.

FULL MOON

4 Paint small gray circles on the white cap as craters.

JUPITER

5 Paint darker or lighter swirls on the orange cap as Jupiter's clouds.

6 When the paint dries, coat all bottle cap tops with clear nail polish. This will help keep the paint from chipping.

7 Squeeze a drop of hot glue into the back of a cap.

8 Stick a pin back into the glue. Repeat steps 7 and 8 with the other caps. Once the glue dries, attach your pins to a backpack or jacket!

GALAXY GEAR

Use heat transfer to make over an old backpack, tote bag, or T-shirt into space-themed gear.

MATERIALS
~ repurposed, light-colored cotton or canvas item
~ string
~ plastic tub
~ ice
~ powder fabric dye in three colors
~ scissors
~ water
~ white paint
~ paintbrush

1 Scrunch, twist, and ball up the item to dye. Wrap and tie pieces of string around the fabric to keep it bunched up.

2 Place the item in a plastic tub and cover it with ice. Make sure the ice stays below the tub's rim.

3 Sprinkle the dye over the ice, switching up colors.

4 Leave the tub in a warm or sunny spot until the ice melts.

5 Remove the item from the tub. Cut the strings from the item and rinse it until the water runs clear. Wash and dry the item to set the dye.

6 Paint white dots and swirls on the item as stars and **comets**.

SWAP IT!
Swap the powder fabric dye for natural dyes! With adult help, boil leftover beet juice, black beans, or coffee grounds into a **concentrate**. Then use it to dye your fabric item.

SURPRISE SOAP ON A ROPE

Use science to turn leftover soap scraps into a like-new bar with surprises inside!

MATERIALS
- ~ leftover glycerin soap bar pieces
- ~ dinner knife
- ~ microwave-safe bowl
- ~ spoon
- ~ recycled paper cup
- ~ small figurines
- ~ rope
- ~ scissors

1 Cut any larger leftover soap pieces into 1-inch (2.5 cm) squares. Place all pieces in the bowl.

2 Microwave the soap pieces for thirty seconds and stir. Repeat until the soap has melted.

3 Have an adult help your pour the soap into the cup. Let the soap cool for ten minutes. Then carefully drop the small figurines into the cup.

4 Cut a 10-inch (25 cm) piece of rope. Knot its ends together and drop the knotted end into the cup.

5 Allow the soap to cool until solid. Place the cup in the freezer for faster results. Then peel the cup from the soap and hang your soap surprise in the shower!

CLOUD CUBBY CADDY

Create a weather-themed locker caddy to store school supplies.

MATERIALS
~ 3 8½" × 11" sheets of felt
~ pencil
~ scissors
~ fabric glue
~ recycled or repurposed string
~ leftover beads from other projects

1 Draw a cloud and a long, thin rectangle on felt. Cut out the shapes, then trace and cut out a second cloud.

2 Fold the thin rectangle into a loop. Glue its ends to the top of one cloud.

3 Next, add rain! Cut strings of different lengths. Glue one end of each string to the bottom of the cloud from step 2.

4 Glue the second cloud on top of the first.

5 Tie beads to the strings as raindrops.

6 Cut a felt rectangle to become a large pocket. Glue the bottom and sides of the pocket to the cloud. Hang your rainy-day caddy up at home or in your locker!

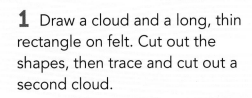

SWAP IT!
Swap the felt for an old T-shirt or towel.

STALACTITE CRYSTAL CANDY

Turn a recycled jar into a science lab! Use heat to turn a sugar solution into candy crystals over time.

MATERIALS
- ~ measuring cups
- ~ water
- ~ saucepan
- ~ sugar
- ~ recycled glass jar
- ~ wooden sticks
- ~ clothespin
- ~ bowl
- ~ food dye
- ~ dish
- ~ food-safe paintbrush or paper towels

STEM Takeaway
Stalactites are mineral deposits that form on cave ceilings. Some stalactites are colorful and look like crystals.

1 With an adult's help, boil 3 cups water in a saucepan. Add ¼ cup sugar and wait for it to **dissolve** in the water. Repeat this step twenty times to add 5 cups of sugar total. Carefully pour the solution into the jar.

2 Soak a wooden stick in water for five minutes, then attach a clothespin to one end to form a T.

3 Pour some sugar in a bowl. Hold the stick from step 2 by its clothespin and roll the stick in the sugar.

4 Lay two other sticks across the jar rim. Dunk the sugar-coated stick in the jar, resting its clothespin on the other sticks.

5 Let the jar sit for three to five days. Check on the jar and watch as crystals form inside!

6 Pull the candy-coated stick from the jar. Mix food coloring and water in a dish. Paint or dab the mixture onto the candy to make the candy look like colorful crystal formations.

RAINBOW CRAYON CANDLE

Melt, reshape, and chill old crayon pieces to turn them into a colorful candle!

MATERIALS
- ~ old crayon bits in white, red, orange, yellow, green, blue, and violet shades
- ~ small recycled glass jars
- ~ wooden craft stick or wooden popsicle stick
- ~ cotton string
- ~ scissors
- ~ large recycled glass jar

STEM Takeaway
Wax is a main ingredient in crayons. Heat turns wax from solid to liquid. Wax becomes solid again when cooled.

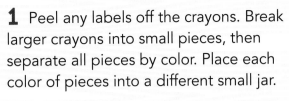

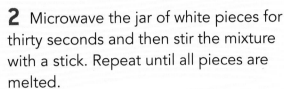

1 Peel any labels off the crayons. Break larger crayons into small pieces, then separate all pieces by color. Place each color of pieces into a different small jar.

2 Microwave the jar of white pieces for thirty seconds and then stir the mixture with a stick. Repeat until all pieces are melted.

3 Cut a piece of string 2 inches (5 cm) longer than the large jar. This will be the wick. Soak it in the white crayon mixture for one minute. Then have an adult use a wooden stick to pull the wick out of the wax and hold it in the air until its wax coating hardens.

4 Tie one end of the wick to the middle of the stick. Rest the stick on the large jar rim so the wick dangles inside the jar.

5 Repeat step 2 with the red crayon pieces. Then have an adult help you carefully pour the red wax around the wick in the large jar.

6 Chill the large jar in the refrigerator for ten minutes. Then repeat steps 4 and 5 using the orange, yellow, green, blue, and violet pieces until the large jar is filled. Gently shake the candle from the jar and trim the wick.

SWAP IT!
Swap the rainbow crayon colors for whatever you have on hand to make a striped candle!

SEDIMENTARY GEMSTONES

Use pressure to turn leftover bits of clay into cool layered stones!

MATERIALS
- ~ leftover pieces of polymer or air-dry clay
- ~ plastic wrap
- ~ rolling pin
- ~ dinner knife

IF USING POLYMER CLAY:
- ~ baking sheet
- ~ aluminum foil
- ~ oven mitts

STEM Takeaway
Most sedimentary rocks are made of materials that have been pressed together. Their formation takes thousands of years in nature.

1 Shape each bit of clay into a ball.

2 Place one ball between two layers of plastic wrap. Use a rolling pin to flatten the ball into a thin disk. Repeat for each ball.

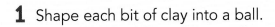

3 Remove the disks from the plastic wrap and stack them.

4 Place the stacked disks between two layers of plastic wrap. Flatten the stack with the rolling pin, using pressure to fuse the clay pieces together.

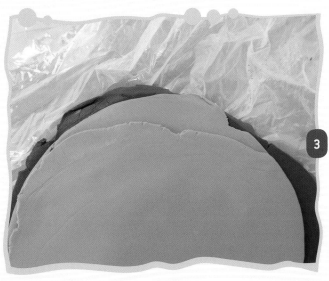

5 Remove the fused clay from the plastic wrap. Use the dinner knife to cut the clay into angled pieces to look like gemstones.

6 If you are using polymer clay, cover a baking sheet in aluminum foil and place the clay pieces on it. Bake the clay according to its package instructions. If you are using air-dry clay, allow the pieces to dry overnight.

STORMY SEA WAVE BOTTLE

Remodel a recycled bottle into a stormy ocean scene to learn about density and waves!

MATERIALS
~ recycled plastic water or soda bottle with lid
~ paint
~ paintbrushes
~ canola or vegetable oil
~ liquid measuring cup
~ water
~ blue food coloring
~ spoon

1 Peel any labels from the bottle, then rest it on its side. Paint storm clouds and lightning on one side.

2 Stand the bottle upright. Fill it halfway with oil. Let the oil settle.

3 Fill the measuring cup with water. Stir in 5 to 6 drops of food coloring.

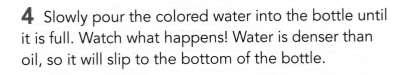

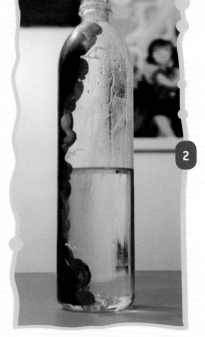

4 Slowly pour the colored water into the bottle until it is full. Watch what happens! Water is denser than oil, so it will slip to the bottom of the bottle.

5 Screw the bottle's cap on tightly and turn the bottle on its side. Gently rock the bottle to make waves.

SWAP IT!
Swap the bottle for a recycled plastic or glass jar with a lid.

FIZZY BATH BOMBS

Mix up a chemical reaction to make bubbling bath bars!

MATERIALS
- 1 box baking soda
- bowl
- citric acid
- cornstarch
- whisk
- spray bottle
- water
- food coloring
- spoon
- recycled water bottles
- craft knife
- scissors
- small figurine

STEM Takeaway
When baking soda and citric acid are combined and added to water, it makes a chemical reaction that creates carbon dioxide. This is what causes these bath bombs to fizz.

1 Pour the baking soda into the bowl. Add 1 cup citric acid and 2 cups cornstarch. Stir the mixture with a whisk.

2 Fill the spray bottle with water. Add a few drops of food coloring.

3 Spritz the mixture from step 1 twice and stir. The mixture may foam a bit, and that's okay. Just keep stirring! Repeat this step until the mixture looks like wet sand.

4 Have an adult cut the bottom third from each water bottle using a craft knife and scissors. Carefully press the mixture into the bottle bottoms until they are about half full. For a fun surprise, bury a small toy in each!

5 Let the mixture dry until firm and no longer crumbly. Then gently remove the bath bombs from the bottles. Toss one in a tub of water and watch the chemical reaction begin!

JAR TERRARIUM

Create a tiny, sustainable ecosystem! The plants will recycle water, oxygen, and carbon dioxide to survive inside a closed jar.

STEM Takeaway

Terrariums are closed areas used for raising small plants or tiny animals. Terrariums are usually made of see-through material.

MATERIALS
~ recycled glass jar
~ pebbles or stones
~ dirt
~ small ferns
~ water

OPTIONAL
~ charcoal
~ small figurines

1 Cover the bottom of the jar with pebbles or stones. These will allow extra water to drain off the plants. If you have charcoal, add a few pieces on top. They will **filter** the water.

2 Pour 2 inches (5 cm) of dirt into the jar.

3 Use your finger to make one hole in the dirt for each fern.

4 Gently place the ferns into the holes.

Jar Terrarium continued on next page

5 Add small dinosaur figurines or other tiny decorative items to your terrarium.

6 Spritz a little water into the jar and screw on the lid.

7 Place the terrarium in a shady spot and check on it over time. The jar may get foggy. This is normal! It means the inside of the jar is warmer than the room. This makes the water in the soil turn to steam. When the steam touches a cool surface, like the side of the jar, it will turn back into water. The water drops will fall into the soil, watering the plants! This cycle will repeat again and again.

8 Open the jar for a day if the soil looks too wet.

ODDS & ENDS

Craft materials and a little creativity can give new life to all kinds of old or recycled materials. What else can you repurpose?

PLASTIC CONTAINERS
Explore the science of music and sound by repurposing plastic food containers with lids into little drums!

PLASTIC BOTTLE
Paint a plastic bottle to look like a space rocket. Cut out rocket fins and a rocket nose from paper and tape them onto the bottle.

MILK CARTONS
Turn an empty milk carton on its side and cut out one long side. Then use the carton as a windowsill planter to grow herbs or flowers.

PLASTIC BAG
Tie strings to the handles of a plastic bag and then around the rim of a plastic cup. This creates a parachute! Test how fast different non-breakable items fall by placing them in the cup and dropping the parachute.

PLASTIC CAPS
Turn plastic caps into tiny boats by gluing a toothpick and small leaf to each as a mast and sail. Place the boats on water and see which one moves fastest in wind.

GLOSSARY

caddy: a container for storing objects when they are not in use

comets: bright celestial bodies with long tails of light

concentrate: food reduced in bulk by removing fluid from it

concept: a general idea

creativity: the use of the imagination to think of new ideas

density: how much mass a substance has in a given space

dissolve: to seem to disappear when mixed with liquid

ecosystem: a connected group of plants and animals and their physical environment

equipment: the tools, machines, or products needed for a certain purpose

filter: to pass liquids or gases through a device in order to clean them

heat transfer: the movement of thermal energy from one thing to another thing of different temperature

repurposed: given a new purpose

solution: a mixture made up of a substance that has dissolved in liquid

sustainable: done in a contained way and which does not use up natural resources

FURTHER INFORMATION

BOOKS

Ardley, Neil. *101 Great Science Experiments.*
New York: Dorling Kindersley Limited, 2014.
Learn the science principles behind these 101 projects you can make at home!

Chatterton, Crystal. *Awesome Science Experiments for Kids.*
New York: Rockridge Press, 2018.
Use the scientific method to complete cool experiments! Photos and instructions guide you through each project.

Felix, Rebecca. *Mini Science Fun.*
Minneapolis: Lerner Publications, 2017.
Create on a small scale! Instructions and colorful photos teach you to use science to make teeny tiny crafts.

WEBSITES

Funology: Science Experiments
http://www.funology.com/science-experiments/
Perform experiments with weather, food, plants, and more!

Martha Stewart: Eco-Kid Projects
https://www.marthastewart.com/274932/eco-kid-projects
Check out eight simple, polished projects made from recycled materials you can find at home!

Science Bob: Experiments
https://sciencebob.com/category/experiments/
Simple directions for completing all kinds of science experiments.

INDEX

ABOUT THE AUTHOR/ PHOTOGRAPHER

Veronica Thompson lives in a little brownstone in Brooklyn, New York, with her two puppies and wonderful husband. She spends her days crafting for her website, makescoutdiy.com, and building websites.